The J-Files

Written by John Parsons

Illustrated by Paul Könye

Contents	Page
Chapter 1. *A secret factory*	4
Chapter 2. *A worldwide disaster!*	12
Chapter 3. *The sound of laughter*	20
Chapter 4. *A brainstorm*	27
Verse	32

Rigby

The J-Files

With these characters ...

Esmeralda
Twinkle

Some J-File
Team Members

"This is the world's

Setting the scene ...

Have you ever wondered who thinks up all the world's jokes?

Now, for the very first time, you will find out! Read about the secret of the J-Files, and how a worldwide joke disaster was stopped.

But remember: don't tell *anyone.* It's top secret!

most secret computer ..."

Chapter 1.

Shhh! You are about to read a J-File! It is top secret. Never tell anyone about this J-File. If kids find out our secret, all our work will be ruined!

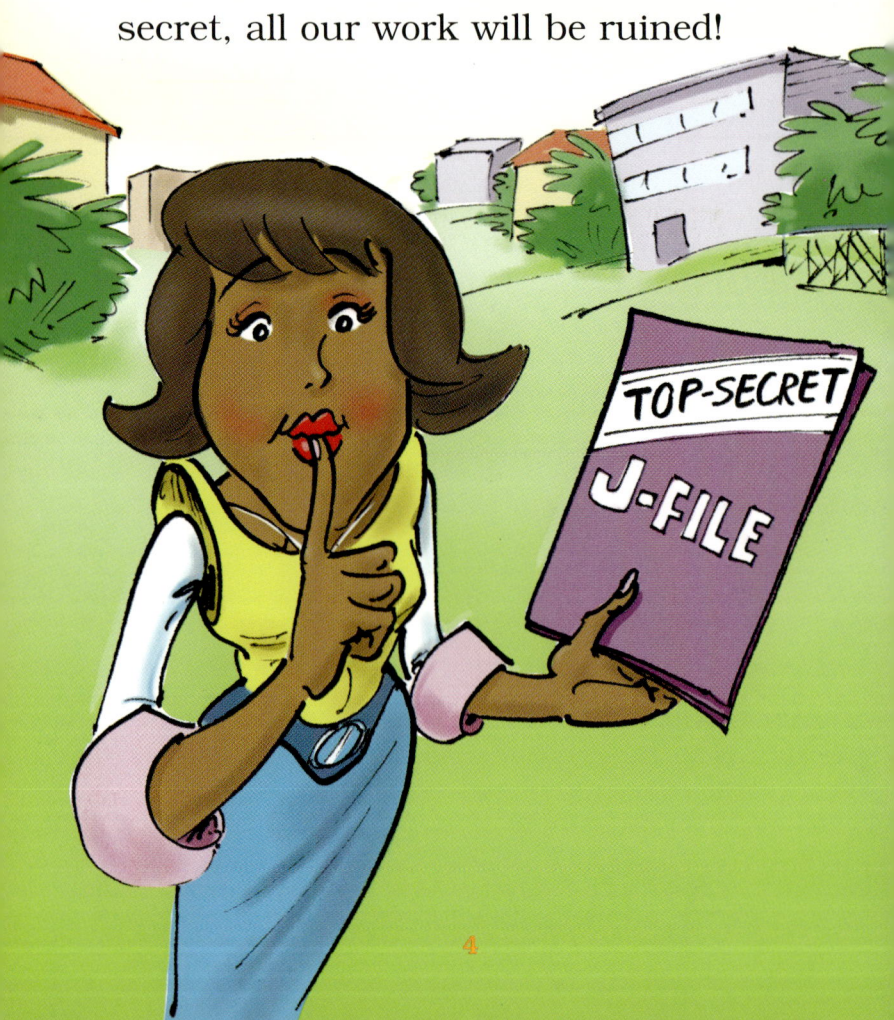

My name is Esmeralda Twinkle.
I work in a factory in Hootsville.
From the outside, it looks like an
ordinary factory. But on the inside,
it doesn't look like a factory at all.
This is where we keep . . . the J-Files!

Instead of hearing factory machines, you can hear a lot of giggling and laughing. Instead of seeing ordinary factory posters, there are hilarious posters on the wall. Tickly feathers hang from the roof, and banana peels lie on the floor.

The J-File team members are paid to be silly and tell jokes. Day after day, that is their job. They think up the world's most hilarious jokes.

If you walk through a long tunnel, you'll find a top secret control room. On one wall, there are huge video computer screens. On one screen, there is a world map. On another, a thick red line goes up and down.

This is the world's most secret computer. It is called the Cheer-o-Meter. It measures how cheerful people are around the world!

If the red line is at Level 1, people are gloomy and glum. If it is at Level 10, people are cheery and happy.

To keep the Cheer-o-Meter at Level 10, we invent new jokes every day. First, we meet to talk about them. After our meetings, we tell as many people as we can about our new jokes.

We call radio stations to tell the jokes to their listeners. We type our jokes onto the Internet. We phone people who write funny TV shows and movies. Very quickly, our new jokes get told all around the world.

For many years, our secret factory has invented the world's best jokes. But one day, something terrible happened to us.

Chapter 2.

It happened at a Monday morning meeting. All our J-File jokers looked gloomy and glum.

"Good morning," I said. "Who wants to tell the first joke?"

No one spoke. For the first time, no one could think of any funny jokes!

"Come on, think hard! Think of something funny, like an elephant tripping over its pajamas. Or what about grandmothers making mud pies to throw at kids," I said. "Just one joke to start the day."

Everyone shook their heads slowly.

"Ple-e-e-ase! Does anyone have even a half-funny joke?" I asked.

Still, no one spoke. The J-File team looked down at their blank sheets of paper. This was awful! We had run out of ideas for jokes.

This could become a worldwide disaster! I ran down to the control room to check the Cheer-o-Meter. The people in the control room were worried. The red line had dropped to eight, the "good" level.

Slowly, the red line moved down to five, the "only just fine" level. Then it dropped down to four (mopey). Then to three (miserable)! The world was short of jokes. This *was* a disaster!

We held an emergency meeting.
We put on feather hats and flippers.
We listened to silly CDs and blew
bubbles in our fizzy drinks.

Still, we couldn't think of any jokes! Then the red line on the Cheer-o-Meter fell from Level three (miserable) to Level two (gloomy).

Finally, we decided to read through our old J-Files. We found some old jokes that might work. Quickly, we phoned the radio stations and typed them onto the Internet.

"What do pigs do after school?
Hamwork!"

"Where do baby apes go to sleep?
In apricots!"

"Why do cowboys ride horses?
Because they're too heavy to carry!"

"What's the difference between
a banana and a lion?
It takes much longer to peel a lion!"

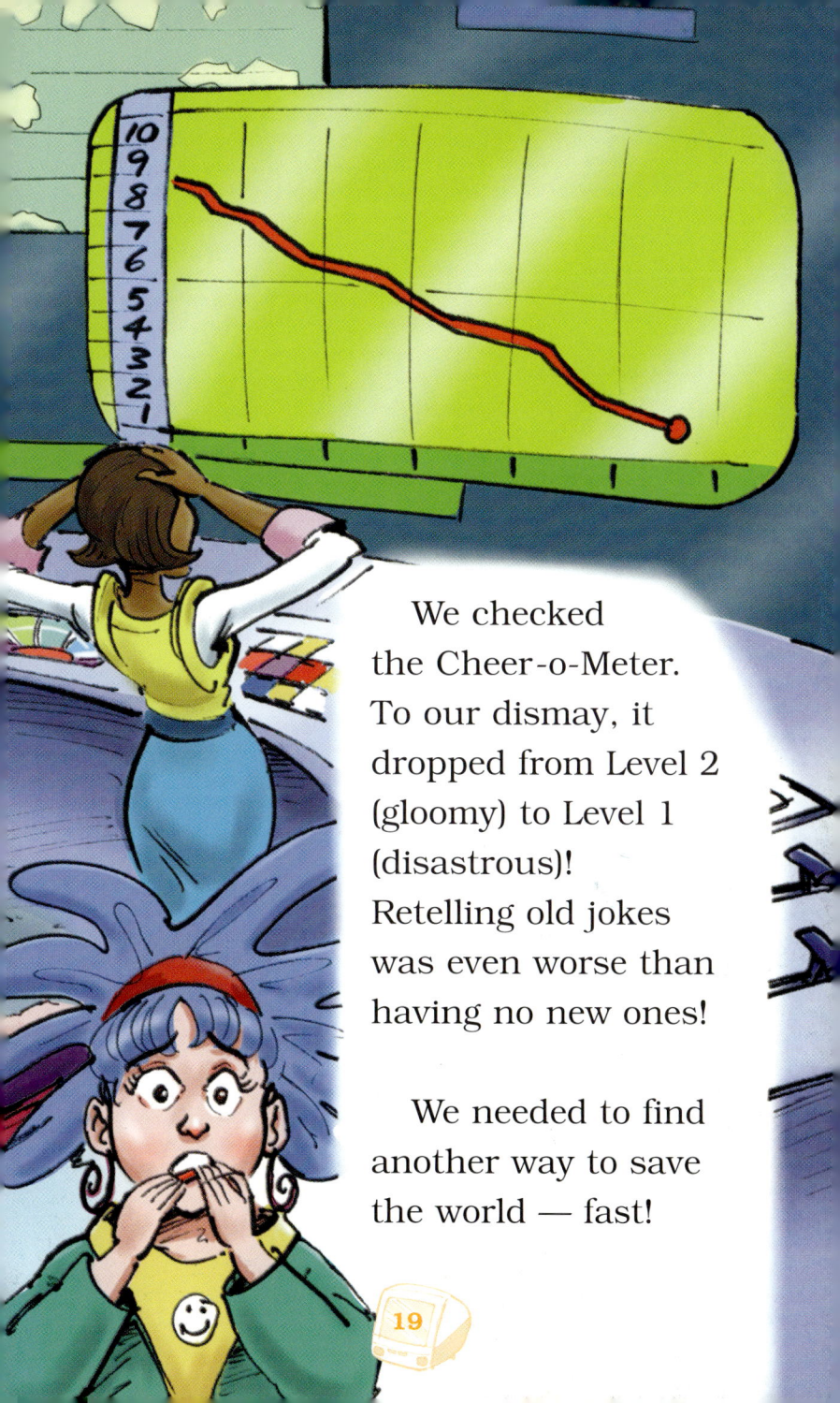

We checked the Cheer-o-Meter. To our dismay, it dropped from Level 2 (gloomy) to Level 1 (disastrous)! Retelling old jokes was even worse than having no new ones!

We needed to find another way to save the world — fast!

Chapter 3.

At midnight I was still in my office. For the first time, no giggles or goofy jokes were heard in the factory.

By the light of my desk lamp, I scribbled jokes about wigs on chickens and kids riding kangaroos. I wished they would make me laugh. But they were just not funny.

I scrunched up the jokes and threw them in the trash. When the sun rose on Tuesday morning, I was surrounded by scrunched-up sheets of paper.

Now I *was* worried. What would happen if the Cheer-o-Meter dropped to zero?

After staring at blank sheets of paper, I looked at my watch. Nine o'clock! I needed to go home for a nap.

As I walked home, everyone in the street was frowning. Angry car drivers blew their horns at each other. A grouchy butcher shook his fist at a dog stealing hotdogs. Without new jokes, this problem was out of control!

Suddenly I stopped and listened. Could it be? Yes! I heard the sounds of giggling and laughing! But where was it coming from?

No one could be laughing, with the Cheer-o-Meter at Level 1. I ran toward the sounds. They were coming from Hootsville School!

I crawled through some bushes and crouched under a classroom window. I heard voices and more giggles. I could barely hear what was being said.

"What do cows eat for breakfast? Moo-sli!"

"How do skunks keep in touch? They call each other on smellular phones!"

I quietly giggled to myself. I hadn't heard those jokes before! Who was telling them?

I peeked over the window sill. Inside the classroom, a group of kids were telling jokes to each other.

"If a dog wants a snack half-way through a video, what will he do? Press the paws button!"

"Why are elephants always wrinkly? Because no one can fit them on an ironing board!"

I scribbled the jokes in my notebook.

Just then, a very grumpy teacher stomped into the classroom.

"Quiet please! No more talking and giggling!" she growled.

The kids stopped. But at least I had overheard four new jokes before that grouchy teacher arrived.

Instead of going home, I ran back to the J-Files factory. Everyone would be arriving for the morning meeting soon. And did I have a surprise for them!

Chapter 4.

I was a J-File hero! Within minutes, the kids' jokes were typed into the computers. We translated them into different languages. We sent them around the world on the Internet. At the switchboard, people called up everyone they knew and told them the jokes.

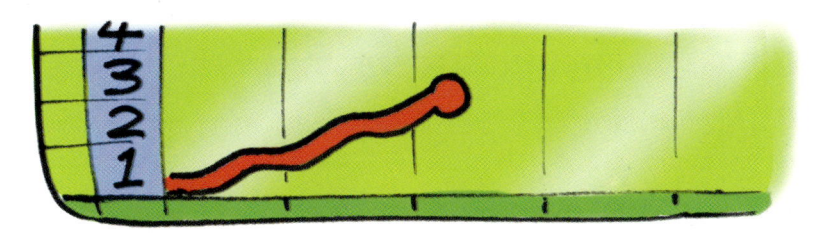

We checked the Cheer-o-Meter screen. Slowly, the red line crept upward, from one to two. Everyone held their breath.

But when it moved from two to three, everyone cheered!

Then I had a brainstorm! I told the others and we made plans.

Early the next morning, when no one was around, a secret J-File team sneaked into the Hootsville School. Under every desk we hid tiny microphones.

Back at the factory, our computer people wore earphones and waited. Soon, the first kids arrived at school. We could hear everything they said! Within seconds, we had taped their jokes. The jokes were typed in, and sent around the world.

On the Cheer-o-Meter's screen, the red line moved even higher. Everyone breathed a sigh of relief.

In the following weeks, our secret J-File team hid microphones in all the schools around Hootsville. Then we hid microphones in all the schools around the country. By the end of the year, we had heard everything that kids said in every school!

Our disaster was over. Every week, hundreds of new jokes were invented by kids. Now the Cheer-o-Meter is always at a cheery and chirpy Level 10.

But remember: you must keep this story top secret. Schoolchildren must not find out about the hidden microphones! If they discover we are listening to every word they say, we'll be in big trouble.

If we run out of funny jokes again, the Cheer-o-Meter may hit zero!

So, whatever you do, don't tell *anyone* about the story in this J-File! If the kids find out, we might never laugh again!

"Under Your Desk"

Some jokes are funny, some jokes are dumb,
Without any jokes, our world would be glum.

Under your desk, our microphone sends
All of the jokes you tell to your friends.

So be careful next time you make them all smile,
Your jokes might end up in a secret J-File!